Scientists who have changed the world

Alexander Fleming

by Beverley Birch

OTHER TITLES IN THE SERIES
Alexander Graham Bell by Michael Pollard (1-85015-200-4)
Charles Darwin by Anna Sproule (1-85015-213-6)
Thomas A. Edison by Anna Sproule (1-85015-201-2)
Albert Einstein by Fiona Macdonald (1-85015-253-5)
Galileo Galilei by Michael White (1-85015-227-6)
Johann Gutenberg by Michael Pollard (1-85015-255-1)
Guglielmo Marconi by Beverley Birch (1-85015-185-7)
Margaret Mead by Michael Pollard (1-85015-228-4)
Isaac Newton by Michael White (1-85015-243-8)
James Watt by Anna Sproule (1-85015-254-3)
The Wright Brothers by Anna Sproule (1-85015-229-2)

Picture Credits
Bridgeman Art Library: 11, 12(below), 15, 16; Edinburgh Photographic Library: 12(top);
Mary Evans Picture Library: 19, 21(top), 28, 29; Nick Birch (Exley Publications Picture
Library): 21(below), 23, 24, 25(right), 32(both), 34, 35(all), 38, 42(top), 43, 47(top),
49(top), 53, 56-7(all); Popperfoto: 7, 40, 59; Robert Hunt Picture Library: 31, 48, 54;
Science Photo Library: 9(both), 25(left), 39, 42(below); Sir William Dunn School of
Pathology: 44, 45, 46-7, 49(below), 50, 51; St. Mary's Hospital Medical School: Cover,
18, 20, 26, 27, 33, 37, 55; The Scottish Regimental Trust: 17; Time Inc.: 5.

Acknowledgements

The grateful thanks of author, photographer and publisher are due to St.
Mary's Hospital: in particular to Charles S.F. Easmon, MD, PhD,
MRCPath, Professor of Medical Microbiology, who so generously gave us
the opportunity to observe and photograph a modern bacteriology
laboratory in the rooms where Alexander Fleming himself once worked; to
Stuart Kessock-Philip, Laboratory Manager of Diagnostic Bacteriology, for
many rich insights into the aims and techniques of the profession; to all those
in the laboratory whose skills are photographed here; and to Nigel Palmer,
Librarian, for help and guidance in obtaining important reference sources.

We are deeply indebted to George L.W. Bonney, MS, for sharing his
invaluable memories of Alexander Fleming and early penicillin work with
him at St. Mary's Hospital, London.

Published in Great Britain in 1990 by Exley Publications Ltd,
16 Chalk Hill, Watford, Herts WD1 4BN, United Kingdom.

British Library Cataloguing in Publication Data
Birch, Beverley.
    Alexander Fleming — (Scientists who have changed the world).
    1. Medicine. Bacteriology.
        Fleming, Sir Alexander, *1881-1955.*
    I. Title.
    II. Series.
    616'.014'0924

ISBN 1-85015-184-9

Series conceived and edited by Helen Exley.
Picture research: Kate Duffy.
Editorial: Margaret Montgomery.
End matter: Samantha Armstrong.
Typeset by Brush Off Studios, St Albans, Herts AL3 4PH.
Printed and bound in Hungary.

Alexander Fleming

The bacteriologist who discovered penicillin – the
miracle drug that has saved millions of lives

Beverley Birch

EXLEY

TIME

THE WEEKLY NEWSMAGAZINE

DR. ALEXANDER FLEMING
His penicillin will save more lives than war can spend.
(Medicine)

The case of Harry Lambert

The man was plainly dying. For more than six weeks they had been fighting to save him. But now his temperature soared. He tossed and mumbled in the throes of a vicious fever, wracked by agonizing spasms and uncontrollable hiccups. And then from time to time he was drowsy, falling into a coma.

To Alexander Fleming, standing by his bedside, there was no doubt that Harry Lambert had little time to live.

Fleming, like the other doctors in St. Mary's Hospital, London, knew what was wrong with Lambert. Microbes – microscopic living organisms – had invaded his body. Diseases like this were usually caused by some form of microbe taking over and weakening or poisoning a person's body, sometimes to the point of death.

They had tried to treat him with the only drugs they had. He had simply become much worse.

And all the time Alexander Fleming had been trying to track down the microbe. Without knowing which it was, the doctors could not hope to save Lambert's life. And so in his laboratory Fleming had worked on determinedly.

At first Lambert had seemed to be suffering from a kind of influenza. But as his condition deteriorated, all the terrible signs of the disease known as *meningitis* began to show themselves. And meningitis, an infection of the waterproof sheath of membranes that surround the brain and spinal cord, was too often fatal.

Using a hollow needle and a syringe, Fleming drew off some of the watery fluid surrounding Lambert's spinal cord. If he had meningitis, then the microbe *must* show itself in that spinal fluid.

And this time Fleming saw it. It was one of the round microbes, which grow in chains, called a *streptococcus*, virulent, fast-spreading, and often

Opposite: An American magazine cover of 1944. Alexander Fleming had discovered penicillin – in the juice of a mould – sixteen years before, in 1928; when this magazine appeared, scientists in Oxford had been working for more than four years to transform that raw juice into the most powerful medical drug ever known. It was not until journalists heard of Harry Lambert that penicillin began to hit the newspaper headlines.

the cause of killer diseases.

Doctors had been having some successes killing *streptococci* with new chemical drugs called *sulphonamides*. But they had used these on Harry Lambert, and he was still dying.

One last chance

There was one last thing to try. Alexander Fleming had telephoned the only person who could help him. In Oxford, Professor Howard Florey was heading a team of scientists who had developed a new drug. It was made from the substance that he, Alexander Fleming, had himself discovered nearly fourteen years before, and named *penicillin*.

Florey's response was swift. He had given Fleming all the penicillin they had in Oxford. It was a very precious supply: there would be none left after Fleming had used this up, not until the Oxford team could make some more. And that was a slow and laborious process that would take months.

Florey had told Fleming exactly how to use it. It was important to know this, for penicillin did not stay in the body very long, and it was vital to maintain the supply long enough for it to do its work.

It was now the evening of August 6, 1942. It was an historic occasion: it was the moment when the man who discovered penicillin – the miracle drug which transformed medical history for all time – first injected it into a patient, and saw its incredible power working before his own eyes.

Watching and waiting

Fleming gave the injection. Three hours later, he gave another. And again three hours later. Right through the night the injections went on, while the nurses, and other doctors, and Alexander Fleming watched.

And as they watched, Harry Lambert became calmer. The hiccups disappeared. And finally he slept.

It was only twenty-four hours since that first injection. Almost in disbelief, the doctors found

his temperature had fallen to normal for the first time in more than six weeks.

They must continue with seven more days of penicillin injections: Howard Florey had made this very clear. It was now August 13.

But Alexander Fleming was becoming anxious, for Lambert had stopped getting better. His temperature was rising, and the delirious ramblings had begun again.

What could Fleming do now? He had found the *streptococcus* in the watery fluid around Lambert's spinal cord. Had the penicillin failed to pass from the man's blood into his spinal fluid, to kill the *streptococci* there?

Again Fleming drew off some of Lambert's spinal fluid into a syringe, and took it quickly to his laboratory. He put the fluid under a microscope and checked for signs of penicillin. There were none.

But if the *streptococci* had not been killed in the spinal fluid, they would be multiplying and spreading, and there would be no hope for Harry Lambert.

Fleming qualified as a doctor in 1906, having studied medicine at St. Mary's Hospital for nearly five years. He wanted to become a surgeon, and while he studied for his next exams he worked in the bacteriology department of the hospital. He so quickly became fascinated by microbes that he never worked as a surgeon. He remained devoted to bacteriology and to St. Mary's Hospital for more than forty-eight years – until his death in 1955.

A life or death gamble

Again Fleming telephoned Florey in Oxford, for Florey's team of scientists and doctors had been testing penicillin for many months. Had they ever injected it directly into someone's spinal canal, the tunnel in the backbone which held the spinal cord? Florey confirmed they had not.

Dare Fleming try it on Lambert? On the one hand there was the chance it might save his life. On the other was the chance it would so badly shock his body, that the injection itself would kill him.

He did not know that even as he made up his mind to do it, Howard Florey also hurried to investigate the problem. He was injecting penicillin into the spinal canal of a rabbit. Nor did Fleming know that the rabbit immediately died.

In London, Fleming carefully inserted the needle between two sections of Lambert's spine, into the spinal canal. The penicillin shot straight into the spinal fluid.

And then he waited. Would Lambert start shivering violently, would his temperature soar, would he vomit, have a fit, or show any of the signs of severe shock at something that had devastated his body? Would he then, instantaneously, die, like the rabbit that Alexander Fleming mercifully did not know about?

Before his eyes, the transformation began. First Lambert's temperature dropped. His delirious ramblings stopped and he became clear-headed. All signs of fever and inflammation faded. His appetite returned. The days went by and he received more injections, again into his spinal canal. This time he simply got better and better.

By all previous medical experience, Harry Lambert should now be dead. A month later, he walked out of the hospital completely cured.

The miracle drug

For those of us who have grown up in a world which has always had penicillin, it is difficult to imagine the excitement felt by Alexander Fleming

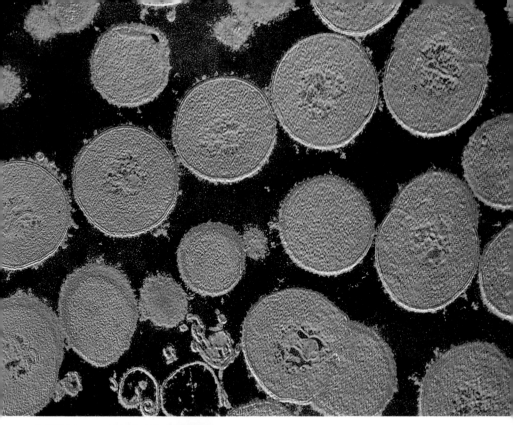

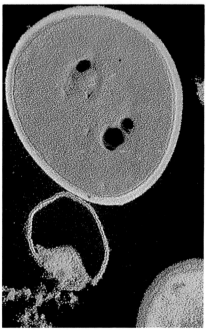

Above: "Streptococci", the kind of microbes which infected Harry Lambert, magnified more than twenty-five thousand times their real size. The microbes known as bacteria multiply by dividing: one organism simply becomes two – and this can happen every twenty minutes. This means that one bacterium entering a human body could multiply to more than one hundred million in just nine hours.

Left: "Staphylococcus aureus", magnified to sixty thousand times its real size. The picture shows a complete bacterium at the top, and another being dissolved by an antibiotic – the type of medicine of which penicillin was the first. The antibiotic destroys the outer membrane (blue around the complete bacterium) so that contents of the bacterium spill out. "Staphylococcus aureus" causes many infections which contain pus, like boils, abscesses and carbuncles. Before penicillin, these infections could be fatal in brains, bones or lungs.

9

and the other doctors and nurses of St. Mary's Hospital when they saw Harry Lambert's transformation from a dying man.

Until the case of Harry Lambert, probably the only people who had felt that tremendous excitement were the men and women of the Oxford team of scientists led by Howard Florey.

They had taken Alexander Fleming's penicillin, purified and refined it. They had worked out by months of trial and error how to keep it in a person's body long enough for it to do its life-saving work. They had seen its power, and were probably the only people who fully understood the importance of transforming the raw juice of a mould into a drug which would save untold millions of lives.

But now, in these August weeks of 1942, the scientist whose unique, sharp-eyed observation on a September day in 1928 had revealed the existence of penicillin, saw the miraculous effect of his own discovery.

The roots of disease

It was little more than seventy years since the work of Louis Pasteur in France had begun to transform scientific thinking and make scientists and doctors alike realize that microbes were at the root of much disease and decay.

Since the first glimmerings of this understanding many scientists, like Alexander Fleming, had been searching for a substance to kill dangerous micro-organisms when they were *inside a person's body*, without harming the body itself.

And some important discoveries had been made. Led by Pasteur's work in the 1870s, it had been found that weakened microbes could be injected as a *vaccine* into people to stimulate their bodies' natural defences. These defences would then be armed against active microbes of the same kind and give the person what we call *immunity*.

Then in the 1930s there had been the dramatic development of several chemical drugs which could be injected into a person. But they didn't always work, and when they did it was only on a few specific micro-organisms.

The vast majority of microbes, once in the body, could rampage through unhindered. Though doctors could now name the culprits, and even, with the power of their microscopes, *see* them in people's body fluids, tissues, and blood, doctors could still do very little about them.

Killer infections

In 1942, a large number of the patients that filled the hospitals were still children and young people suffering from infections caused by one or other of the dangerous microbes. Too often these infections led to death. Women died in childbirth or infants died shortly after birth. Children died from scarlet fever, from infections of the bones, throat, stomach or brain. The microbes invaded wounds, causing a spreading infection that could kill a person in a few days. Even an infected pin-prick or a tiny cut might be lethal.

A mother, weakened by an uncontrollable infection, is unlikely to survive the birth of her child. Her newborn baby would have little chance of survival: millions of children died each year from invasions of bacteria. Hospitals were full of people suffering from infections that the doctors could not control: in 1900, tuberculosis – caused by a microbe – killed fifty-three thousand people in Britain alone.

Nowadays children frequently receive antibiotics, for example for infections of the ear, throat or chest. Before penicillin, they might have died on any of these occasions.

Above: Lochfield farm in Scotland, where Alexander Fleming was born and lived during his early childhood.

Alec's father leased the farm from the local landowner, and here he herded sheep and cattle and grew some crops.

Right: On the farm the pattern of the year followed the seasons: spring lambing, early summer shearing, cutting peat for fuel, haymaking for the hard winter. Harsh cold could devastate the livestock, and Lochfield was buffeted by vicious gales and snow blizzards that could bury the sheep in minutes.

A thing of the past

Many doctors today will never have seen the kinds of diseases which filled the hospitals only fifty years ago. They are now a thing of the past.

We owe that to the dawn of the antibiotic age – the era of drugs made by using one microbe to kill another. We owe it, therefore, to the man who discovered the first – and still the best – antibiotic, penicillin.

And we owe it to the men and women of the Oxford team whose work twelve years later made it possible to use Alexander Fleming's penicillin as one of the most powerful medical drugs ever known.

In 1945, Alexander Fleming, for his discovery of penicillin, shared the Nobel Prize for Medicine with the two scientists who headed the Oxford team that gave penicillin to the world – Howard Florey and Ernst Chain.

Childhood in the Ayrshire hills

Alexander, or Alec, as his family called him, grew up in a place very different from the crowded, noisy streets, smoke and dirt of London where he spent over fifty years of his working life, and where he made his life-saving discovery.

It was among the windswept hills and glens of the uplands of Ayrshire, in the south-west of Scotland, that he was born and spent the first fourteen years of his life.

He was born on August 6, 1881, in a remote farmhouse in the hills four miles from the small town of Darvel. Above the farmhouse stretched rough pastureland, and beyond, the wide, wild expanses of heather-covered moors.

The Fleming family was a large one. Their father's first wife had died leaving four children, and he had married again when he was sixty. With his new wife, Grace, he had four more children, and Alec was the third of these.

Alec's father died when Alec was seven, and it was his eldest brother, Hugh, and his mother who brought up the family and ran the farm.

Alec's early life was full, free and outdoor. The pattern of daily life for the older children followed the care of the animals and household chores – fetching water from the spring and fuel for the fire. But the younger boys had little work to do except for some sheep-minding. Alec was able to spend his days in the company of his brother John, two years older than himself, and his brother Robert, two years younger. They played in the barns, roamed the farm and moors, explored the streams, which formed waterfalls and deep cold pools in the glens, and fished in the river waters.

Schooldays on the moors

Alec's schooling also took place among the hills, for when he was five he went to a little school on the moors a mile from Lochfield. Here a young teacher taught some nine or ten children from the nearby farms, gathered in the single class-room or, in fine weather, by the river.

In later life, when he was world-famous, Alec still said that the best part of his education was in that tiny moorland school, and the daily walk to and from it. It was certainly true that the young Alec learned to be fascinated by nature and developed a keen eye for observing and remembering everything around him. They were qualities which would one day reveal the existence of penicillin.

In 1891, when Alec was ten, he and Robert moved to the school in nearby Darvel, a small lace-making town that extended along the floor of a green valley on the Upper Irvine river. It was a four-mile walk away. But the two boys strode along through all weathers, four miles there, and four miles back each evening.

At twelve, instead of the small, familiar communities of Lochfield and Darvel, Alec had to face a big secondary school in Kilmarnock, an important industrial town of some thirty thousand inhabitants.

But in the summer of 1895, there was a dramatic change in his life. For some time their mother and the elder brothers, Hugh and Tom, had been worrying about the future of the younger boys, John,

Alec and Robert. When their father died, he had left the tenancy of the farm to Hugh, who ran it with their mother. Tom had gone on to study medicine at Glasgow University.

Now the family wrestled with the question: should the younger boys remain on the farm, like Hugh, or should they follow Tom's example, continue their education and look for other ways of earning a living?

In the end it was Tom's life that provided the answer. By 1893 Tom, now qualified as a doctor, had set up medical practice in London, treating eye problems. His eldest sister, Mary, had gone to keep house for him. Tom invited John to join them, and found him an apprenticeship in the firm of lens makers that supplied Tom in his work.

Now, in the summer of 1895, the invitation came to Alec too. Tom suggested he come to London to finish his schooling.

So it was that thirteen-year-old Alec Fleming left the open spaces of Scotland and entered the bustle, noise, and industrial smoke of London. He little realized that this enormous city would be his home for the rest of his life.

A street in the old City of London when thirteen-year-old Alec came to London in 1895. He settled with his brothers in a house shaken by the rumble of steam-driven trains on the underground railway passing nearby. His first job, lasting four years, was as a clerk in a shipping office in this part of London.

15

The crowded London streets held unending fascination for the brothers reared on the Scottish farm. Alec was the ring-leader of their escapades in London. Well-trained by the years roaming the moors, they walked vast distances to see the sights of London and rode the top decks of the open buses in all weathers.

London

The pleasure of London was vastly increased when, six months later, brother Robert joined them. Now the trio of boys, who had together roamed the moorland wilderness, were reunited. John learned the trade of lens-making, and Robert joined Alec at the Regent Street Polytechnic, which provided classes for a small fee for anyone wanting to learn.

By the time he was sixteen, Alec had passed all his exams. But he had no strong feelings about what kind of work he wanted to do, so he took a job in a shipping office of the America Line, a company that ran some of the largest and fastest of the liners across the North Atlantic.

As a junior clerk Alec had to copy documents by hand, keep accounts and record details of cargo and passengers. He worked carefully and well, but he found it very dull. In the four years he spent there, there was no hint of the future, quite different, path his life would shortly take.

The legacy

In 1901 there came an unexpected opportunity for Alec. An uncle had recently died and left each of the Fleming children a legacy.

Dr. Tom Fleming at once used his legacy to open a consulting room in London's Harley Street, and he rapidly began to get many more patients. By this time Robert had joined John in the lens making firm. Both of them liked the work, and seemed well settled. When they received their money they set up their own firm of lens makers, which, in time, developed into a large company with many branches. In 1942, it was a director of this firm, Harry Lambert, whose recovery from near death would give Alec Fleming such pleasure.

But for all Alec's hard work at his clerical job, Tom could see he was not enjoying it. On the other hand, medicine was proving to be a secure and interesting profession for Tom himself. He began to wonder whether this would offer better opportunities for his young, unsatisfied, brother.

He put the proposal to Alec. Why not use the legacy to study medicine and become a doctor?

New directions, new vistas

Alec liked the idea. It offered a way out of the boredom of the shipping office. Yet it was a formidable task he faced. He was nearly twenty, several years older than most first-year medical students. He had none of the qualifications needed for acceptance by a London medical school, for he had left formal school at the age of thirteen and a half.

But he set out to obtain the qualifications he needed. He found a teacher to coach him in the evenings, and by July 1901 he sat the exam. He

Alec in the uniform of the London Scottish Rifle Volunteers. In 1899 volunteers were asked to join part-time military regiments. They were needed to support the regular British army in the Boer War against the Dutch settlers (the Boers) in South Africa. Alec and his brothers joined the London Scottish Rifle Volunteers.

They never served in South Africa, but they stayed in the regiment. It was a place where they could meet friends and learn new sports. They became skilled with rifles. One day this would place Alec firmly on the path to the discovery of penicillin.

passed in all sixteen subjects. And so in October 1901 Alec Fleming joined St. Mary's Hospital Medical School. He little realized that this hospital would claim him for the whole of his working life, nor that here he would become one of the most famous scientists of all time.

A world of knowledge

Alec settled quickly to his new life in a world so different from the record-keeping of his clerical work that the years spent in the shipping office seemed never to have happened. Now he had to investigate the structure of the human body, its tissues and organs, in the minutest detail.

And he also had to study how the different parts worked, although most of what we now know about the detailed processes inside the body were still undiscovered at the time Alec was a student.

He had taken up medicine just to escape clerical work. But he soon found he had stumbled into a profession that thoroughly suited him. There wasn't

A lecture in St. Mary's Hospital. Alexander Fleming is in the front row to the left of the gangway. The students learned also through practical experience in the hospital. They lanced boils and drained abscesses, stitched cuts and dressed wounds, extracted teeth and strapped up broken bones. But there was little doctors could do to treat many of the diseases that filled the hospitals in these decades before the discovery of antibiotics.

a subject he didn't enjoy: and he became well-known among the students for winning prizes for his work.

Life was not all study, however. Energetically he entered the community life of the hospital. He played water polo, joined the Dramatic and the Debating Societies and became a star member of the rifle club.

In July 1904, when he was twenty-two, he passed his first medical exams. He was beginning to feel that he would like to become a surgeon.

With the first exams behind them, the students no longer spent their time in lecture rooms and classes, but in the wards and casualty rooms of the working hospital. They would trail through the wards behind a doctor to watch how he examined patients. They had to learn what to look for, and how to put together a picture of a patient's illness so they could recommend treatment.

The limits of medicine

There was a great deal to learn. But for all that, there was actually very little the doctors at that time could do to treat many of the diseases that filled a hospital like St. Mary's.

It was only nine years since X-rays had been discovered, and would be several decades more before St. Mary's had an X-ray department. Doctors knew the parts of the body in detail. But exactly how these parts worked together, and what they actually *did,* was little understood.

Scientists had only just begun to unravel the mechanism by which the body fights off disease. And no one could really do anything against the vast battery of microbes that could attack the human body, causing devastation and often death. The battle against the microbes had scarcely begun.

But of all the places he could have chosen to study medicine, Alec Fleming had unknowingly selected one where some of the most exciting work was being done. One of his teachers was a pioneer in this new war against disease-causing microbes. His name was Almroth Wright.

Dr. Emile Roux, who developed one of the few great medical successes of the time – a treatment for diphtheria. This killed thousands of children annually in most countries of Europe. They were attacked by a poison – a toxin – produced by the microbe in the body. The treatment was made from the blood of horses made "immune" by repeated injections of toxin, stimulating their bodies to fight it. But this was success in an otherwise dismal picture. Most of the development of vaccines and "anti-toxins" was still to come.

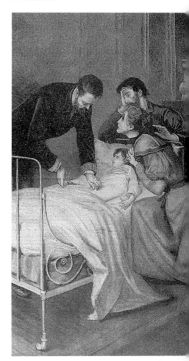

Almroth Wright

As a young man in the 1880s, Almroth Wright had studied in Europe under some of the great medical scientists of the time. It was a very exciting, fast-moving period in science in Europe.

Microbes had been observed and recorded since the seventeenth century. But the work of Pasteur from the 1850s onwards had driven scientists forward in a great surge of activity. In the 1870s Robert Koch, a German scientist, first proved that a single disease is caused by a specific microbe.

In laboratories all over Europe, scientists looked for new ways of handling and studying microbes, particularly the class of microbes known as *bacteria*. Intricate techniques of staining bacteria were developed, so that they could be more easily watched and tracked in their movement.

Almroth Wright observed and learned. He took this knowledge back to Britain at a time when little of these developments was altering medical practice there.

Later he worked at an army medical school. He became particularly interested in wound infection by bacteria, and in diseases like cholera, typhoid and dysentery. These often attacked armies at war: crowding and dirt combined to give a perfect environment for the bacteria which cause these killer diseases to flourish.

Above: Almroth Wright, the single most important influence in Fleming's working life, and one of the great pioneers in the war against dangerous microbes.

No cures

For diseases like these there were still no cures, although Pasteur's work in the 1870s had begun to reveal the direction of advance. He had shown that by injecting a vaccine made of bacteria that had been *weakened* in some way, doctors could force the body's natural defences to arm themselves.

But this idea had not yet been very widely accepted in Britain. Almroth Wright became one of the great pioneers of vaccine therapy, and a fierce campaigner for it. By the time he became Professor of Pathology and Bacteriology at St. Mary's Hospital in 1902, he had come to believe passionately that the right vaccination could do much more than

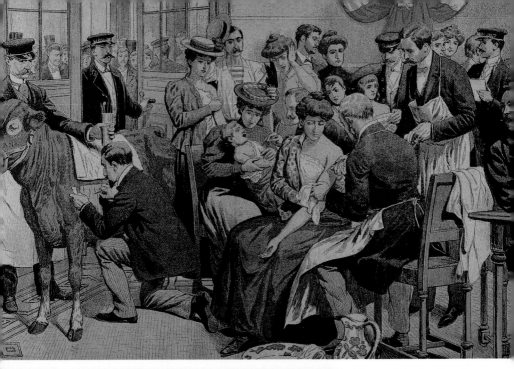

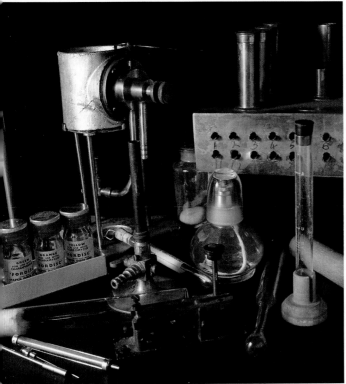

Above: Vaccination for smallpox had been used for a hundred years. But in this, the body's defences against the microbes of a mild disease – "cowpox" – were used against a serious disease, "smallpox". Pasteur showed a different line of attack. By injecting weakened bacteria you could force the body to arm itself against the same bacteria in their active state. This was what Wright was developing.

Left: Laboratory equipment of the time. Wright and his team were working on the frontiers of medical knowledge, developing techniques and apparatus as they went.

prevent bacterial diseases. He was certain it could also *cure* them.

Alec Fleming was one of the students caught up by the excitement of Almroth Wright's lectures. Wright was an astonishing man, dazzling in style, forceful in ideas, and already with a gigantic reputation for fighting for the cause he adopted.

Alec was greatly impressed by these new vistas in the war against bacteria. But he didn't yet think of becoming a bacteriologist. Surgery was still his main aim, and he had taken the preliminary exam in January 1905.

A year later, in July 1906, shortly before his twenty-fifth birthday, he passed his final medical examinations. He was now a qualified doctor. He could begin to practise either in St. Mary's or another hospital, or in a general practice of his own, like his brother Tom.

But what he wanted to do was stay in the medical school and work for a higher exam to give him greater choice for the future. The problem was that he didn't have much money. He needed to earn a living in some way and also find the time to continue studying.

The Clarence Wing of St. Mary's Hospital, as it is today. From 1908 it housed Almroth Wright's laboratories as well as the wards for patients being treated with his vaccines – the first research wards in Britain. Fleming worked here until the 1930s when the laboratories were moved into a new building.

Chance, and the rifle club

By chance, there was someone in the medical school who particularly wanted to keep him there. This was John Freeman, a keen member of St. Mary's Rifle Club. That year the rifle team hoped to win an important national contest. Alec was a significant member of the team, so Freeman set out to keep him busy at St. Mary's, to make sure he would still be around for the contest.

Freeman was also a member of Almroth Wright's department, and knew that Wright had a vacancy for a junior assistant. He suggested Alec.

So it was that in the summer of 1906 Alexander Fleming joined Almroth Wright's department. It was meant to be a temporary solution to his problem. He was soon so engrossed in his work that he remained a member of that department for the rest of his working life.

Early work in bacteriology

At this time Almroth Wright was forty-five years old and at the height of his career. He had an enormous reputation for his pioneering work, much influence and some powerful friends, including some in the British government.

His enthusiasm infected his whole department. Eight or nine young graduates, Alec among them, fell to the work with great energy. They were convinced they were going to bring a revolution in medical science.

They often worked long into the night if crucial measurements had to be taken on an experiment. At tea time each day they gathered for an animated discussion, and again at around midnight, when they reviewed the day's work. The department hummed with activity.

Alec fitted in easily, though at first quietly. But his general good nature and interest in all that was going on, soon made him well-liked. His practical skills began to show themselves as an enormously valuable resource for the department. Everyone who knew him at this time talks of his deftness and skill with his fingers.

The work often involved intricate practical problems – how to manipulate or measure minute amounts of substances. Alec would listen to Almroth Wright explain some new idea, without saying a word would disappear to his laboratory bench and return after a few hours with some neat new tiny gadget or an intricate method that exactly solved the problem.

The library at St. Mary's Medical School, as it is today, and as it was in Fleming's day. Generations of medical students study in these halls, heirs to a very different medical world because of Fleming's discovery of penicillin. Fleming himself was also a teacher, Professor of Bacteriology from 1928.

The body's natural defences

The department was absorbed in investigating what vaccination did to the body's defence system, what we call the *immune* system. What exactly happened when a vaccine was injected? How did the body react? What processes took place that made the body then able to fight off a disease?

Wright believed passionately in the importance of the *natural defences* of the body against bacteria. His idea was that to control bacterial disease (curing

Above: Alexander Fleming's microscope: the microscope was at the heart of all study of microbes. The most basic task was to identify a microbe present during an infection, and prove whether it was the cause. Then the search for a weapon against it could begin.

as well as preventing) you had to stimulate the body to *make itself invulnerable.*

But no one knew much about the natural defence or *immune* system of a body. The members of Wright's department were trying various ways to force it to work, and then trying to observe and measure what was happening.

They would, for example, identify the bacteria they believed were causing a disease, grow them, kill them, mix them in a fluid to make an injection, and then make sure that each measured amount of this vaccine had exactly the same number of bacteria in it, so developing a "standard" dose.

They injected the vaccines into animals, patients or themselves. Then they looked at drops of blood from the injected person, under a microscope. They tried to record and measure what had happened to it, how different it was from the blood of a person who had *not* been injected.

Phagocytes, the swallower cells

They had become very interested in one part of the blood – the white blood cells known as *phagocytes.* This simply meant "swallower cells" because these cells actually swallowed and digested bacteria.

They looked at phagocytes in ordinary blood. Then they looked at phagocytes in the blood of someone who had recovered from infection or been given one of the vaccines. For a long time, Wright was convinced that there was a special sort of substance in the blood of these people that encouraged the phagocytes to swallow bacteria.

He called this substance *opsonin,* and the department spent much energy and many midnight hours trying to record and measure what they believed was opsonin at work.

It seemed to all of them that they were pushing back the frontiers of medicine.

The year of decision

By 1908 Alec passed his next exams with distinction and a Gold Medal. He decided to work for the specialist examination which would qualify him as a

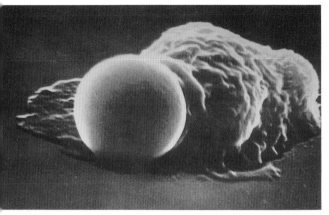

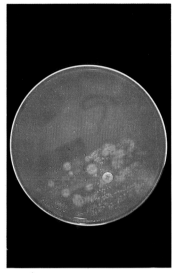

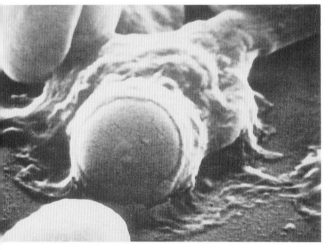

Left: A white blood cell – a phagocyte – nearing, engulfing and consuming a red blood cell. Phagocytes also remove foreign particles like microbes from the body: it was this that interested Wright's scientists.

Above: A natural mix of different bacteria. Bacteriologists spread a sample of a patient's blood, urine or saliva across a "culture medium" on which bacteria grow easily. Each bacterium multiplies into a visually distinct colony – as shown here. Some are harmless inhabitants of the body. Some may be dangerous. The bacteriologist lifts the colony to be studied onto a clean "culture dish", to grow on its own. On the dish shown here, one type of bacteria has dissolved the red blood cells in the culture medium – as shown by the pale areas.

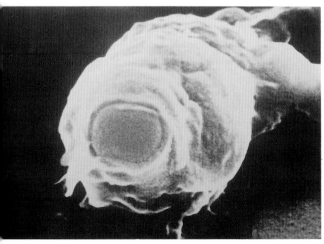

Fleming's persistent, thoughtful and untiring study from the age of twenty-five was dedicated to the search for ways to overcome the ravages of infection on the human body.

surgeon, and get practical experience in the hospital as Casualty House Surgeon. By June 1909, at the age of twenty-seven, he had passed the exam.

Now was the moment, when, with all his qualifications, he could begin work as a surgeon.

But he decided instead to remain with Almroth Wright. He had become totally absorbed by the work. His brother Robert recalled how the family noticed this shift in Alec's interest. He stopped talking about surgery and spoke a lot more about Wright's ideas. He even started trying them out on the family. Sore throats, colds, any kind of minor infection would prompt Alec to take a sample of mucus or blood back to the laboratory to look for bacteria, reappearing with a vaccine which he would duly inject into the long-suffering "patient".

Dr. Fleming's reputation grows

As his work continued, Alec won a reputation as an expert on vaccine therapy. He also made a name for himself in one particular field. He had developed a much better test, using just one or two drops of blood, for the terrible disease of *syphilis.*

This is a devastating illness, known in history as "the pox". Untreated, it destroys the body slowly over many years, and can be passed on by a mother to her unborn child. It was particularly difficult for doctors to tell whether someone was suffering from it, because the spiral-shaped bacteria that cause it were difficult to isolate. But they could detect that the bacteria were there because of changes in the blood. So Alec's improved test was important, and many patients came to him for it.

A wonder drug

In these years there was one great leap in the treatment of syphilis and Alec was one of the first to use it. It began in 1910.

In Germany, a scientist named Paul Ehrlich was trying to make chemical substances that would be more poisonous for microbes than for people. He wanted to find a "magic bullet" to hit only the microbe it was sent against.

He tested 605 chemicals and found one very poisonous for the bacteria which cause syphilis, but much less harmful for people. He called it "606", and later "Salvarsan". It could be given by injection so that it reached every part of the body and found the bacteria wherever they lurked.

Almroth Wright knew Ehrlich, and was one of the first to get a supply for testing in Britain. He asked Alec and another doctor in the department, Leonard Colebrook, to try it out. They used it with great success, and Alec began to win a considerable reputation as an authority on treating syphilis.

War

But in 1914 this work was abruptly interrupted and Alec was transported many miles from the familiar walls of St. Mary's to a hospital in France. World War I had begun.

Almroth Wright had fought long and hard for his typhoid vaccine to be given automatically to soldiers at war. With the outbreak of this war he lost no time, at once offering the services of his department to the army.

All troops must be injected against typhoid immediately, he insisted. More than that, wound infections must be treated with the new vaccines he was developing. He still believed that weakened bacteria should be injected into patients to stimulate their own immune system to fight wound infection.

Without Wright's vaccine, there would probably have been at least 120,000 deaths in the British Army from typhoid over the four years of World War I. Instead there were only 1,200.

But army doctors were not convinced that Wright was right about vaccines for wounds. They suggested he set up a research unit at a war hospital, and find out.

The Casino in Boulogne

October of 1914 found Wright, Alec, John Freeman, Leonard Colebrook and several other bacteriologists from St. Mary's surveying the grim misery of hideously-wounded men from the battlefields.

Private 606: a cartoon by an artist friend of Alec's. It shows Alec in the uniform of the London Scottish Rifle Volunteers, holding a syringe of 606. Well-known for using the new drug 606 against syphilis, Alec would later himself discover the substance that would become, and remain, the most effective and least dangerous treatment of this disease – penicillin.

27

Above: In the trenches of World War I, mud, blood and dirt, damp and overcrowding combined to give perfect conditions for deadly microbes to spread. Some of the most dangerous produce spores – tiny "seeds" – that can survive, perhaps for years, and burst into life when conditions are right. One is the tetanus microbe. It produces a poison that causes terrible spasms in the muscles, usually killing the victim. There was no remedy against the microbe that causes gas gangrene except to cut off the infected limb.

The hospital was in the grand Casino in Boulogne. Beneath elegant chandeliers, where once the rich had played, rows of campbeds held groaning and bleeding soldiers. Many had been waiting days for surgery. Their wounds were sickening, filthy and usually already infected. Often the culprits were a variety of common bacteria, but sometimes the dreaded *gas gangrene* had taken over.

This was caused by a virulent microbe, spreading with terrifying speed, poisoning the wound and blackening the surrounding muscles and skin, filling it with gas in a few hours. The only treatment was to cut off the limb. This might save a man: delaying would mean certain death.

The doctors could only pour chemicals known as antiseptics into the wounds and try to kill the

bacteria. They had been treating wounds like this since the Scottish doctor, Joseph Lister, introduced the first antiseptic in the 1860s.

The quest for the perfect antiseptic

When he read about Pasteur's work in 1867, Lister decided that bacteria must be causing the infections that usually followed surgery in hospitals. He began using a substance called *carbolic acid* to keep equipment, air and surgical wounds free of bacteria.

He transformed surgery, not just because other doctors began to use carbolic as an antiseptic, but also because they began to understand the need for cleanliness.

But when it came to killing bacteria in an *already-infected* wound, the problem was not so easy to

Above: A first-aid station in World War I. The conditions in which Wright's unit had to work were appalling: at first a few rooms in a basement, stinking with leaking sewage. Then rooms with no gas, water, or drainage. They constructed a makeshift laboratory, supplied water and drainage with pumps and cans, and got to work.

29

solve. How could you apply antiseptics and not damage the tissues of the body? Lister tried diluting carbolic acid so as not to do a great deal of harm to anything but the bacteria; but for years he went on searching for a chemical that would destroy bacteria without harming living human tissue at all. He never found it.

Over the next seventy years, many other workers launched on the same quest. But it was only after Alec Fleming discovered penicillin, that the quest would come to fruition.

Now, as Wright's unit began work in Boulogne, doctors in general and army doctors in particular still had an unshaken faith in chemical antiseptics for treating wounds. Yet liberally pouring on chemicals did not usually have the result they wanted. The infection invariably continued, or even got much worse.

And no one knew what these substances were actually doing to the body tissues, particularly deep in the wound.

Alec's war years

Why didn't antiseptics work? Which bacteria were causing infections? What was happening in the blood during infection, and what then happened when antiseptics were poured on?

And most curiously, why did antiseptics that worked in a test tube in the laboratory not work in a real wound?

These were the questions that Wright, Fleming and the others set out to answer. Steadily they gathered information, trying to put together a full picture of what was happening. They found out, for example, that the men's clothing was the worst source of bacteria.

And they made a particularly important discovery. In fresh wounds, or untreated ones, the seeping fluids and blood were *full* of phagocytes, all busily swallowing bacteria.

But in wounds where doctors had used antiseptics, there were very few phagocytes. Those they could see were dead or dying. But the bacteria, which the antiseptics were supposed to kill, were still very much alive and multiplying rapidly.

Here, before their eyes, was evidence of something they all believed, and had believed for years. The body's own phagocytes were *vital* to fighting off bacteria. And the antiseptics used by doctors killed the phagocytes.

Alec's artificial wound

Again Alec's clever adaptation of techniques was very valuable. He suspected that antiseptics on the surface also couldn't work because they literally *couldn't reach* into all the torn channels of the wounds.

He made an artificial "wound" from a test tube. He heated the tube to soften the glass, and then shaped it into hollow spikes, like the tunnels of a jagged wound. He filled this with infected liquid, emptied and refilled it with antiseptic. And he showed that the bacteria started spreading again because the antiseptic had never reached deep into the spikes to kill them all.

With all the evidence they collected Wright began his campaign to change the treatment of wound infections. Antiseptics should not be used, he insisted. The wound should only be rinsed with a strong salt solution which would encourage the phagocytes to do the main work, and then protected from new bacteria by clean dressings.

But these ideas were years ahead of the thinking of most doctors of the time. Sadly the work of the dedicated team of bacteriologists in Boulogne did not change most doctors' work in World War I. It was only during World War II that methods like those they put forward began to be used.

The killer influenza

The years of war work made an indelible impression on them all. They struggled to master the infections, but one fact faced them, impossible to avoid. They could do nothing to save most of the wounded who passed through their hands.

Below: Soldiers with artificial limbs. Alec and other scientists and doctors struggled to control the infections rampant in the horrifying conditions of World War I. But there was little they could do to save the lives or the limbs of the men they treated. Antiseptics poured on the surface of the wounds did not destroy the infection deep down. Usually they killed the phagocytes vital to the body's own defence system.

Above: Germ paintings by Alec. He enjoyed playing with bacteria, as well as studying them. These were made with bacteria that turn red and yellow as they grow. Everyone who knew him mentions not only his deftness at his work, but also his obvious enjoyment of it. Once he used his glass-blowing skills to make a glass cat and scampering mice for the entertainment of students visiting him in the laboratory.

Just before the end of the war, they also saw the ravages of an epidemic disease. In 1918 an influenza epidemic hit all the countries of Europe. While doctors were helpless to stop it, over twenty million people died. Young, healthy people felt slightly ill one day, and were dead the next. Far more died of influenza than died in the war itself.

The military hospitals were filled with victims. Wright's unit, particularly Alec, struggled to work out why a usually mild disease had suddenly become such a killer.

But there were no real answers yet, and again the same devastating fact: there was no way of killing bacteria without also killing the body's tissues and phagocytes.

Sareen

As the epidemic subsided, and with the war over, the team's time in Boulogne came to an end. In January 1919, Alec finally returned to the Inoculation Department at St. Mary's Hospital. But it was not a return to his old way of life.

During one of his brief periods of leave from Boulogne, Alec had done something so completely unexpected that at first no one would believe it. He had to show them a photograph to prove it was true. He had got married.

Before the war he had become friendly with two sisters, twins named Sally and Elizabeth McElroy. They were nurses who ran a private nursing home.

Sally, who later became known as Sareen, was an energetic, outgoing person. She talked and laughed a lot, and was so different from Alec, (well known for never saying much and listening a great deal), that friends decided this was probably what drew them together.

They were married in London on December 23, 1915, although Alec, now thirty-four, returned to France immediately after the wedding, and Sally continued running the nursing home. Not long after, the bond between the Flemings and the McElroys was strengthened when Sally's sister Elizabeth married John Fleming.

But Alec's married life could only begin properly in January of 1919, when he returned to England. In 1921, Alec and Sareen bought the Dhoon, a country home set in fine trees, and (particularly to Alec's liking) a large garden with a river where they could swim, boat and fish. From now on the Flemings spent much time at weekends perfecting their large home. When their son Robert was born in 1924, Sareen began to spend more time there, often joined by the children of Alec's brothers, Robert and Tom. The Dhoon became a major focus of their life together, and many happy years were spent there.

Fleming's first great discovery

1921 was an important year. From the twenty-first of November, Alec Fleming's notebooks record the first of his two great discoveries, his natural antiseptic, lysozyme.

Above: The Dhoon at Barton Mills in Suffolk, Alec's country home from 1921. Many threads of his life, broken by the war, had to be picked up when he returned to England. Alec and Sareen began to spend holidays with friends in Suffolk, enjoying the gentle countryside, so different from the hubbub of London. On one of these holidays they bought The Dhoon on an impulse, when they went to an auction there.

He had been busy growing a wide variety of micro-organisms, and observing how they behaved, particularly their reactions to different substances. The search for the perfect antiseptic was always in his mind.

There was a standing joke between Alec and a young doctor who was working with him. Dr. Allison, Alec teased, was much too neat and tidy. He cleared up his bench at the end of each day, busily discarding growths of bacteria he no longer wanted and cleaning the dishes for further use.

By contrast, Alec's bench was crowded with bacteria growths (known as cultures) from experiments over many weeks. He liked to leave them for a while and then have a good, long look at everything before he dumped them in disinfectant. You never knew when something interesting might happen.

One day, he was looking through the piles of old culture dishes, preparing to clear them away. Suddenly he stopped. He peered at one carefully for some minutes, and then showed it to Dr. Allison, saying no more than, "This is interesting."

Alec had been suffering from a cold some weeks earlier, and in his never-ending search for greater

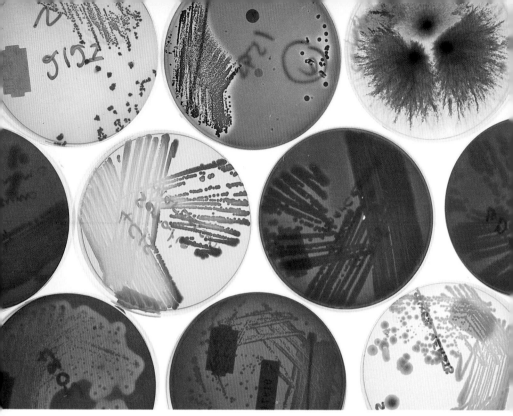

Above: Colonies of different bacteria grown on culture dishes. These have been found in body fluids taken from patients. Bacteriologists must identify the ones that are causing infection.

Opposite: above, left: Alec developed tests for the effect of different substances on bacteria: small pieces of paper soaked in test fluid, inside wells cut in the culture medium. He sowed bacteria on the surface, and could see if they stopped growing as fluid seeped out of the wells. Here a bacteriologist uses a modern version – paper discs soaked in various antibiotics.

understanding of bacteria and disease, had started to grow a blob of the thick fluid from his nose. It was this dish that he showed to Allison.

But what had caught his attention, and what Dr. Allison now saw, was that there were also colonies of golden-yellow bacteria growing on the dish, everywhere *except immediately around the blob of nose fluid.* Next to this they had started growing, but had become glassy and seemed to be dissolving. They were growing normally only *some distance* from the nose fluid.

Despite his few words, Alec was greatly excited. He had seen the significance. Could there be something in the nasal fluid that actually *killed* bacteria?

The body's natural antiseptic

Quickly and carefully, he tested fresh nasal fluid. The same thing happened: the bacteria would not grow near it.

Did it happen with other people's nose fluid? He

Above: Bacteria being studied must be protected from other bacteria which might land by accident. Otherwise scientists cannot be sure which bacteria are causing which effect. Here a bacteriologist is sterilizing a metal "loop" in a flame to kill bacteria that may be on it from the air, bench, hands, clothes or other bacteria cultures in the laboratory. The clean loop can then be used to spread a sample from a patient onto a culture dish, or to transfer a colony of bacteria from one dish to another.

pestered friends and colleagues for samples. It did. And it happened even when they didn't have a cold.

What about other body fluids? He insisted that people cry for him, and hurried away with their gifts of tears; he tested saliva, pus, blood serum – the clear fluid that seeps from a blood clot. All had this amazing ability to stop these golden-yellow bacteria from growing!

Left: A colony of bacteria on the end of a loop.

For years, Alec Fleming had trodden the paths of research laid down by Almroth Wright. But here was something new, something unknown, something he had found himself. Was it some previously unrecognized part of the body's *immune system,* something that worked together with the phagocytes to combat bacteria?

During the next weeks Alec's excitement is shown by the pages of his notebooks filled with more experiments: which body fluids, and which parts of the body had this bacteria-dissolving substance? Which bacteria would it kill?

It seemed to be everywhere! Skin, mucus membranes, most internal organs and tissues, even hair and nails had it. He also found it in some animals, and in plants, flowers and vegetables.

But he found that it only affected some bacteria; most of the dangerous ones were barely affected at all. We now know that Alec had discovered the body's first line of internal defence. If the bacteria could get past this, then the phagocytes had to move into action.

It was in fact the body's natural antiseptic. But at the time the full significance of this was not understood, and it took many more years of research before the processes of this defence system were properly recognized. And because it didn't deal with the very dangerous bacteria, there was little interest among scientists at the time.

Lysozyme was the name Alec chose for the new substance, and he continued investigating it for many years. It was not the work that would shoot him to fame, but he always felt that this was the period of his best and most enjoyable research.

He published many reports about lysozyme, along with Allison and other young bacteriologists who worked with him over the years. But no one really grasped the significance of it, and Alec Fleming was not a man to force their attention.

A "rather interesting" mould

Those who worked with him during this time remember him bent busily and happily over his laboratory bench. His door was always open to visitors and a gossip. Often he would wander into the main laboratory to see what was going on among the younger scientists, and chat about the work or about some general topic of scientific interest.

Then, on a September morning in 1928, Alec Fleming wandered, as usual, into the main laboratory. He was holding a culture dish, and had an air of carrying something rather interesting. They all had a look, but most of them assumed that he was just showing another example of lysozyme at work, though from a mould.

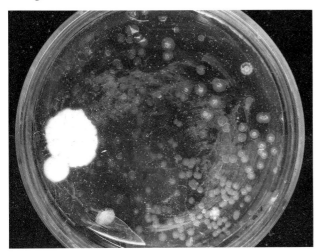

Left: The original culture dish, on which Alec first saw penicillin. To the left is the colony of mould – penicillium. The juice, penicillin, was seeping from this. Immediately to the right is the area in which the colonies of "staphylococci" bacteria were transparent and obviously dissolving. At the far right are the "staphylococci" colonies growing normally – out of reach of the penicillin.

It was not until fourteen years later that they understood, when Florey and Chain in Oxford had fully revealed the power of the mould that Alec held in his hand that September day of 1928. Only then did those young scientists in the St. Mary's laboratory cast their minds back to that faded memory, and try to reconstruct their first sight of penicillin.

The mould that held a miracle

Alec had seen something which escaped the others who peered at his culture dish that day. The mould had done something that the familiar lysozyme had never done.

It had attacked one of the most common and

most dangerous bacteria, the virulent round *cocci* which grow in clumps like bunches of grapes, known as *staphylococci*.

The events of the discovery have been told and retold many times, and are often much embellished by fantasy, not fact. The full story has to be pieced together from Alec's published report at the time, his descriptions many years later, (after the Oxford team had turned penicillin into a powerful drug), and the laboratory notebooks of Alec and his assistants.

The story is extraordinary enough because it is so like Alec's finding of lysozyme. In the same way, he had been sifting through old culture dishes before cleaning them. On that historic occasion in 1928, he was chatting with an assistant named Pryce.

Poisonous!

Pryce had left the department to take up other research. But he dropped in to see how the work he had done with Alec was getting on. They had been growing *staphylococci* from boils, abscesses, nose, throat and skin infections. Then they had left the bacteria at room temperature to see how they changed and how changes altered their strength.

Now Alec was clearing away the cultures of several weeks back. He had inspected and piled most of the dishes into disinfectant for cleaning. He picked one from the top of the pile, not yet covered by disinfectant, to show to Pryce.

And it was then, as he looked at it again, that he paused. He murmured simply, "That's funny", and passed the dish to Pryce.

What Pryce saw were the usual smooth, dome-like colonies of golden-yellow *staphylococci*. They covered the dish – except to one side. There, near the edge, a patch of fluffy mould had started to grow, and near to this, the colonies of *staphylococci* were transparent. Quite close to the mould there were none at all.

Like the other people Alec showed the mouldy plate to that day, Pryce thought little about it until, years later, he realized the full significance of what he had seen.

Below: Bacteria are very adaptable and can develop resistance to penicillin. This is one of Alec's early culture dishes, testing the effect of a substance which some bacteria produce to stop penicillin from attacking them. This substance is called "penicillinase". On the top half of the dish the staphylococci have been able to grow under protection of penicillinase which is also spread on the culture medium here. At the bottom, where there was no penicillinase, the penicillin (middle) has stopped the staphylococci from growing.

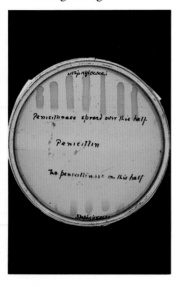

But Alec was already, inwardly, very excited. Something had killed *staphylococci!* He even photographed the dish and preserved it. It is kept to this day in the British Museum.

He lost no time in trying to make the same thing happen again. He put some of the mould onto a fresh dish, and grew it, and then tried to grow *staphylococci* alongside it.

He couldn't. There was no doubt – something seeping from the mould was poisonous to *staphylococci.*

Harmless!

Over the years Alec had tested many substances which could kill bacteria. Now he followed this well-trodden path even more eagerly. One by one he did the same battery of tests on the mould juice. Did it kill other bacteria? Did it harm the phagocytes of the blood? Did it damage the delicate tissues of the human body?

The results were astounding. His mould juice could stop some of the most dangerous bacteria from growing. An unknown mould, landing by chance on a culture dish, could apparently simply dissolve them!

And it didn't harm the body – the phagocytes were still busily at work. Even when the juice was *injected* into the body of a mouse and a rabbit, there were no ill effects. Even when it was heavily diluted, it was lethal for the virulent bacteria!

He had found something vastly more powerful than carbolic acid, yet harmless to the delicate living blood cells!

But he later discovered some serious problems. Most chemical antiseptics killed microbes within a few minutes. The mould juice took several hours. And it seemed to lose its power completely in mixtures that had blood serum in them.

This was very disappointing. It meant that in wounds or infected areas which seeped serum, the mould juice would lose its power long *before* it could kill the bacteria. He did not know then that the Oxford team would solve these problems over

Below: The penicillium mould, "penicillium notatum". Others had observed the effect of penicillium moulds in the past. But these observations came to nothing, until Alec saw his mould in 1928. It was by far the most powerful, and unlike many others, not poisonous for the human body. The world owes an enormous debt to Alec, a scientist so sharpened in the search for a safe weapon against bacteria that he recognized what he saw, recorded, tested, and most of all, preserved his mould.

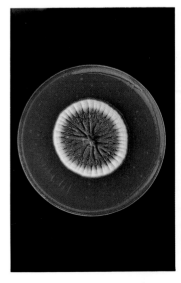

Above: The fluffy growth of "penicillium notatum". Alec, Ridley and Craddock, tried different kinds of culture media for growing the mould. It grew best on the surface of a kind of meat soup at room temperature. As the layer on the surface formed, the liquid below turned more yellow and stronger in its power to kill bacteria. They poured it off and filtered it to remove debris. Lastly they forced it through a very fine filter with a bicycle pump. The remaining clear yellow liquid had most of the bacteria-killing power, but also water and other substances from the soup. They now had to remove all these, leaving the penicillin behind.

eleven years later and launch penicillin on its path from a *mould* juice with unusual powers to a drug which would change medicine for all time.

Penicillin

Another scientist who knew about moulds told him that his was one of the *penicillium* group. Now, in February 1929, Alec began using the name "penicillin" for his bacteria-killing substance.

He became a fanatical collector of moulds. He couldn't, at first, believe that his was the only one with this extraordinary power. His mould quest became famous among family and friends: cheese, jam, old clothes, boots and shoes, old books and paintings, dust and dirt of all kinds, at home, in friends' homes – nothing was safe from Alec's hunt for interesting scrapings he could carry back to test in his laboratory.

But his mould *was* the only one: the more he found out about it, the more extraordinary it seemed. It could even kill the bacteria that caused the hideous gas gangrene he had fought so desperately and so ineffectively in those grim years of World War I.

Trying to purify it

He asked two assistants, Ridley and Craddock, to produce mould juice for his experiments, and find out more about it. They grew the *penicillium* in a kind of meat soup in large bottles with flat sides. Over several days it spread over the surface of the soup in a fluffy layer, while the liquid below turned yellower and yellower, and became more and more powerful in its bacteria-killing effect – its *penicillin*.

But they had difficulty trying to isolate the penicillin from the liquid and other things in the juice. And when they did partly succeed, there were new problems: it very easily lost its bacteria-killing powers! Again it would be the Oxford team, years later, who would finally solve the problem of extracting penicillin in a pure form from the juice.

The "weed-killer" for vaccines

But in the early months of 1929 one thing particularly caught Alec's attention. Penicillin killed many bacteria, but not all. It did not harm the bacterium that scientists believed at the time was the cause of influenza. It was called *Pfeiffer's bacillus,* and was difficult to isolate.

Alec at once saw an important use for penicillin. He could use it to *purify* influenza vaccine, like a "weed-killer", killing all bacteria *except the Pfeiffer's bacillus* he wanted to isolate and cultivate. The memory of the great influenza epidemic and twenty million victims was only ten years old. The search for a weapon against influenza was ever present in Alec's mind.

He also discovered he could use it to isolate other bacteria like those causing the childhood disease of whooping cough.

This use, in the laboratory for selective growing of chosen bacteria, allowed penicillin to emerge as the first great antibiotic drug. Alec kept his penicillium mould going, producing juice week after week for vaccines. Scientists around the world asked for samples to use in isolating the difficult influenza bacteria.

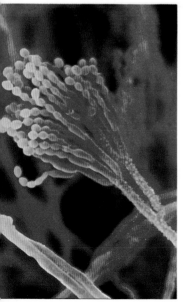

And so the mould that had been sighted by one person, on one occasion, in one laboratory, became established in other laboratories, busily performing its bacteriological work, and waiting for the time when its miraculous role as an antibiotic would be revealed.

The failure to purify penicillin

In the next few years there were two other attempts to extract penicillin and find out more about it. Both attempts faltered at the problem that Ridley and Craddock had already faced: at a certain point in the effort to purify it, its bacteria-killing powers seemed simply to disappear.

But by 1938, in Oxford, the men who would solve the problem, Florey and Chain, had begun working together. They were investigating another substance very dear to Alexander Fleming's heart,

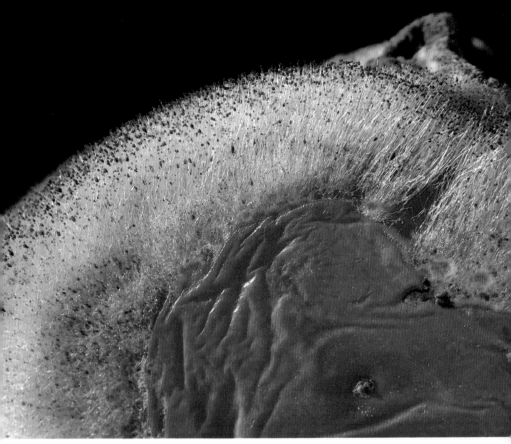

his body fluid antiseptic, *lysozyme*.

The climate of science in which they turned to penicillin was very different from that in which Alec had discovered it or others had tried to purify and investigate it. In the years between Alec's observation in 1928, and the beginnings of Florey and Chain's work on penicillin eleven years later in 1939, scientists in Germany had made a gigantic, revolutionary advance in the treatment of bacterial disease.

The sulphonamides

Ever since Ehrlich had developed Salvarsan in 1910, scientists had been trying to produce chemicals that would kill bacteria by injection into the body, just as the dye, Salvarsan, killed syphilis bacteria.

Then, in 1935, a scientist named Gerhard Domagk announced he had discovered a group of dyes that, by mouth or injection, protected mice

Above: Common moulds growing on an orange (left) and a tomato (right). Far left: The penicillium mould that causes the blue veins in some cheeses, magnified over one thousand times. The picture shows the spores in long chains – each can separate and become a new organism. Moulds grow naturally on all kinds of substances, and Alec could not at first believe that his was the only one with the power to kill dangerous microbes.

from the killer *streptococci*. The one that worked best was a rich red dye called Prontosil.

Used on people, it was as successful, not least for the terrible infection of puerperal fever which struck down, and all too often killed, women after childbirth.

The moment that news of Prontosil broke, other scientists began trying to make similar substances, and it was not long before a group of drugs known as *sulphonamides* was developed. Some of these worked well, and lives were saved in treating dangerous *streptococci* infections like scarlet fever, pneumonia, ear infections and meningitis that doctors had never been able to treat before.

But there were problems with the sulphonamides. They didn't attack all bacteria, and those they did could develop a resistance against the drugs. And even the best could have unpleasant side effects, ranging from skin rashes and violent vomiting, to others that were sometimes fatal.

Howard Florey

Howard Florey became Professor of Pathology in the William Dunn School of Pathology at Oxford University in the year of the sulphonamide revolution, 1935. He was an Australian medical scientist who had come to study at Oxford in 1921, as a young man of twenty-three. He had fast won a substantial reputation for the quality and imaginative range of his research on the detailed internal functioning of different parts of the body.

In 1929 he had become interested in finding out exactly how the stomach worked. He was particularly intrigued by the power of the stomach fluid known as mucus to kill some bacteria. He remembered that in 1922 Alexander Fleming had reported the discovery of the natural antiseptic *lysozyme* in body fluids including stomach mucus.

At once Florey became intensely interested in finding out precisely how *lysozyme* worked, and this line of research lasted some eight or nine years. In 1938 it brought him into the scientific partnership with Ernst Chain, the young scientist who would

Howard Florey, Professor of Pathology at the William Dunn School in Oxford, and head of the Oxford team that produced penicillin as a drug. He was not only a fine scientist, but also a great organizer who saw and used the special talents of his fellow workers. He inspired confidence and enthusiasm, welding them into a dedicated, determined team. For his work on penicillin, he was jointly awarded the Nobel Prize for Medicine in 1945, with Ernst Chain and Alexander Fleming.

win the Nobel Prize with Florey and Fleming.

By this time the sulphonamide revolution had planted new ideas firmly in scientists' heads. They had begun to understand that infections could be best attacked *not* by pouring antiseptics directly onto the infected tissues of the body, but by injecting bacteria-killing substances straight *into the circulating blood* – that is, by using them *systemically.*

A whole new attitude flourished among doctors and medical scientists alike. It launched them on an even more energetic search for better and better systemic weapons in the war against bacteria.

Florey and Chain take up the search

In 1938, as their lysozyme work drew to an end, Florey and Chain discussed going on to a study of other *natural* bacteria-killing substances. Chain searched scientific publications from all over the world and found about two hundred reports on bacteria that scientists had seen stop other bacteria growing. One was Alec's 1929 report on penicillin. Florey and Chain chose three to investigate. One was penicillin.

They got a sample of the *penicillium* mould from a laboratory along the corridor at the Dunn School. It was being used there (as in many other labs) for isolating selected bacteria. And they set to work to find out more about it.

It was not long before they faced the same problem that had defeated earlier attempts to separate the bacteria-killing substance from everything else in the mould juice. At a certain point in the process of isolating and extracting it, the penicillin seemed simply to disappear!

Dark days for the Oxford team

The story of their struggle to solve this, then to produce enough pure penicillin to test on animals and later on people, is a marathon of ingenuity, imagination, persistence and scientific skill. It deserves its own story – not just of Florey and Chain, but also of the other men and women in the team.

Before long they had transformed the William

Ernst Chain, the scientist in Howard Florey's team who succeeded in purifying penicillin where earlier attempts by others had failed. He managed to produce a sufficiently pure penicillin that could be injected into the human body. It then dispersed through the bloodstream and reached all bacteria. For his penicillin work he was joint winner of the Nobel Prize with Florey and Fleming in 1945.

Dunn School of Pathology from teaching and research laboratories into a penicillin production factory. Oil cans, food tins, dustbins and domestic
baths, hospital bedpans, milk churns, coolers and
library bookracks, all were sucked into their
mammoth effort to produce enough mould juice
for their work.

In the first dark months of World War II, as the
people of Britain dug air-raid shelters, suffered
food, fuel and clothing rationing, and there was
evacuation from cities to areas less likely to be
bombed, the Oxford team began work.

Not one of them then had the slightest idea that
penicillin would have any effect on winning the war.

By the middle of March 1940, Chain had won his
first penicillin battle. He had extracted enough to
start testing it on animals. He had 100mg in the
form of a brown powder, much stronger than Alec's
crude mould juice. But to their enormous excitement, it still did not harm animals, phagocytes, or
living tissues in the body.

By the end of May, Florey was ready to do one
experiment which Alec had not done. He had to
find out if penicillin, injected, could *cure* a fatal

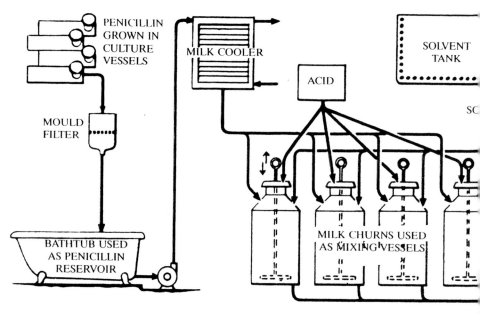

infection in animals.

He knew that penicillin took over four hours to kill bacteria in a test tube. He knew it was passed out of the animal body, in the urine, in only about two hours. But for him the only answer was to try: he prepared the crucial test to see if it could work *systemically,* despite this time-lag.

The crucial experiment

That morning of Saturday May 25, 1940 was their first glimpse of the climb to a new era in medicine. At 11 o'clock Florey injected eight white mice with a deadly dose of *streptococci.*

Four were put back in their cages. Two of the other four were injected with single doses of *penicillin;* the remaining two were given five smaller doses over the next ten hours.

By the following morning the four mice which had *not* been treated with penicillin were dead. The four which had received penicillin were very much alive.

They repeated the tests. They did different tests. They performed endless experiments to find out

Above: Ways of testing antibiotics: front, cylinders (filled with antibiotics) developed from Oxford methods. Left, a later version, and also modern soaked paper discs.

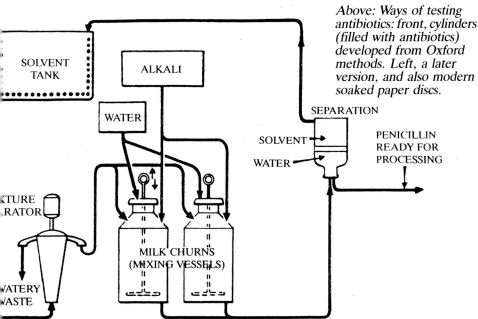

Below: Sheltering from bombs in the underground railway in London during World War II. Against this grim background and the threat of invasion by the Germans, the development of penicillin continued without faltering. Florey and his team made careful arrangements for an emergency departure from Oxford: they smeared spores of penicillium mould in the linings of their coats: they could abandon everything in Oxford, but if they had the spores they could grow new penicillium cultures and start again elsewhere.

what penicillin could and could not do in the body; how precisely it should be given, how often, for how long, in what doses. They were long weeks when Florey and his assistant James Kent slept in the laboratory, waking every three hours to inject one batch of animals, inspect others, and record every detail.

By July, they had completed their experiments. They reported the results in the medical magazine, *The Lancet,* on August 24, 1940. It was, although few people then knew it, the announcement to the world that a new era was dawning. As the death toll in the war mounted into millions, penicillin would begin to save numbers beyond counting.

From mice to people

A human being is three thousand times as big as a mouse. For the Oxford team the challenge loomed enormous.

To treat a person, they would need three thousand times the dose for a mouse. Yet vast amounts of mould juice were needed for minute amounts of penicillin. They calculated that they must produce five hundred litres of mould juice *each week for several months* to get enough penicillin to treat five or six patients. How could they possibly produce such a quantity with their makeshift equipment?

It seemed an impossible hurdle: until they had enough penicillin to prove its effectiveness on people, no drug firm would start producing it. And without help from a firm to produce it, they might never have enough to do the critical human tests.

But they pressed on. They turned the Dunn School into a factory: in one class room six "penicillin girls" used paint sprays to distribute mould

Left, top: Bottles of Chain's "brown powder" – penicillin. The raw, filtered mould juice was of the same strength as Fleming's had been. By a lengthy process of extracting penicillin from other substances in the juice, Chain produced this brown powder in 1940, which was much more powerful. But two years later, purified commercially, penicillin was more than sixty times stronger than this brown powder: in fact 99.9% of the Oxford team's first successful penicillin preparation was not penicillin at all, but unwanted rubbish!

Left, bottom: Bath-tub production at the Dunn School. They needed to make five hundred litres of mould juice each week for several months to provide enough penicillin to treat five or six patients. They used every container they could find to grow the mould – oil cans, biscuit tins, flasks, flat-sided bottles and bedpans!

Above: The "penicillin girls" sowing the penicillium mould in the culture vessels under controlled, germ-free conditions. They used paint sprays to put the mould spores into the vessels. By this time the team had discovered that the mould grew best in ordinary hospital bedpans. Heatley designed a special container based on the shape of the bedpan, and Florey persuaded a manufacturer to make six hundred of these. You can see these on the racks in the picture: they would be kept at a steady temperature for fourteen days, before the juice would be poured off.

spores in the culture vessels. In another the vessels were incubated at just the right temperature while the juice developed. In others, the seven scientists and ten assistants of the Oxford team worked day and night to extract and purify enough penicillin to treat a handful of patients for a few days each.

Alec goes to Oxford

The first that Alec Fleming knew of the Oxford penicillin work was when he read about the animal experiments in *The Lancet*. He lost little time in going to see it. On the morning of September 2, he arrived at the Dunn School.

We can only guess at the pleasure he felt when he saw what the Oxford team were doing with penicillin. With his usual economy of words, Alec said very little, and looked a great deal. Florey showed him around, explaining everything in great detail, and gave him a sample of their penicillin.

Back in London, Alec in turn sent Florey some cultures of *penicillium* mould that produced a good yield of crude penicillin. He wrote enthusiastically, "It only remains for your chemical colleagues to purify the active principle, and then synthesize it, and the sulphonamides will be completely beaten."

By the beginning of 1941, the "factory" in Oxford had enough penicillin to plan their first human test. The penicillin was twice as strong as the samples they had used on animals.

The first human patient

On February 12, 1941 they treated their first patient. He was a policeman Albert Alexander, infected by a rose-bush scratch. *Staphylococci* and *streptococci* had overwhelmed his face, scalp and eyes. Massive doses of sulphonamides had not helped.

Within twenty-four hours of the first penicillin injection there was a dramatic, unmistakable improvement. But Albert Alexander was to be the tragic proof that penicillin must be maintained in the body long enough to do all its work.

The bacteria in the policeman's body were not completely conquered. Despite a period of steady improvement in his health, they began to overtake again. This time, there was no penicillin left to treat him. He died on March 15.

The first success

The second patient was a fifteen year old boy dying of infection after a hip operation. With penicillin, he recovered completely. Six more patients treated with penicillin left them in no doubt. Every one improved dramatically; two were snatched from almost certain death.

But even this, Florey knew, was not enough to convince the world: he felt at least one hundred patients must be treated. Yet they knew now that about *two thousand litres* of mould juice would be needed to treat just *one* severe case of infection.

The USA begins production

He was still unable to get help from British drug firms. He turned instead to the USA. There he managed to stimulate interest enough for production of mould juice to begin in an agricultural research laboratory in Peoria, Illinois.

Margaret Jennings worked alongside Howard Florey on the use of penicillin in the animal and human body. Years later, after his first wife, Ethel Florey, died, she married Howard Florey. Ethel Florey was the doctor who performed the second human trials of penicillin. Other women scientists in the Oxford team wielded their special skills: Jean Orr-Ewing concentrated on testing the effects of penicillin on different microbes.

The Oxford team, however, never got the penicillin from these efforts. In December of that year, the USA entered the war. At once the Americans foresaw the importance of penicillin in treating battle wounds, and all production was geared to the American war effort for battle casualties.

Once again the Oxford scientists were thrown back on their own efforts. They prepared to collect enough penicillin for a second set of medical tests. These, performed during 1942, proved penicillin's miracle powers beyond doubt. Fifteen patients had infections so serious that doctors believed them beyond hope. Treated with penicillin injections, all but one recovered completely.

In one case, the bacteria developed a resistance to penicillin, and the patient died.

Alexander Fleming and Harry Lambert

It was in August of 1942 that Alec Fleming experienced these excitements for himself. This was when Harry Lambert was pulled back from the brink of death by penicillin which Alec himself injected at St. Mary's Hospital in London.

Until the case of Harry Lambert, Alec had not seen the evidence of the Oxford penicillin at work. But something of his amazement and excitement in these years can be gleaned from the memories of George Bonney, a doctor who worked alongside him later, in 1943. At this time St. Mary's received a supply of Oxford penicillin, to be tried out on patients.

George Bonney was Alec's Resident Medical Officer, or "House Surgeon", for the trials. Now, forty-five years later, he remembers the first sight of penicillin's power with the clarity of yesterday.

Penicillin trials at St. Mary's

Their first case was a little girl. She was suffering from an acute infection of the bone by *staphylococci*. Her temperature had soared to 106°F (40°C), and she was dying. George Bonney remembers clearly the cloudy yellowish fluid of the massive penicillin injection they had to give her, every three hours, throughout day and night.

"She was plainly dying," he recalls. "The next morning she was plainly going to live. It was the first time I'd seen such a thing. I shall never forget it. It was an absolute miracle."

And he remembers too, with that same sense of wonder, the other great miracle of penicillin. They were all so used to seeing the side effects of the sulphonamides. Yet here was something that did no harm at all. Pump it into the body, or pour it onto open wounds and there were no problems. There was one hideous eye infection in new-born babies. It had always been untreatable, and could lead to complete blindness. Yet now they could simply drop penicillin onto the eye and watch as the grotesque swelling and seeping pus simply disappeared.

Care and caution

And George Bonney tells how, even gripped by enthusiasm after successes like these, Alec never ceased in his care as a bacteriologist.

He had years of work on antiseptics and sulphonamides behind him; he knew a lot about the

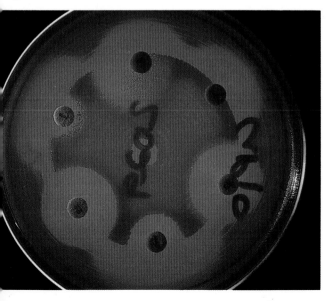

A culture dish showing the effect of different antibiotics on bacteria. Each paper disc is soaked in a different antibiotic, and in the middle of the dish is the bacteria being studied. Around the edge of the dish is the "control bacteria" – whose reaction to the antibiotics is known. The sensitivity of the bacteria in the middle is measured by the size of the lighter area around each disc, where none of it is growing – the "zone of inhibition". Bacteriologists can compare these with the zones around the control bacteria. Where the bacteria has grown right up to the disc, it shows that it is resistant to that particular antibiotic – that is, the antibiotic would have little or no effect.

infinite capacity of bacteria to adapt and develop resistance to the weapons used against them. Now he was conscious from the start of such dangers in the use of penicillin.

Penicillin, he was determined, must be carefully and thoughtfully used. They must not help resistant strains of bacteria to develop. Before Alec allowed penicillin to be used on an infection, they must first confirm that the particular bacteria were vulnerable to the drug. Only then was it right to use on a patient.

And even in these early days, Alec predicted wider use, in surgery, not least wound surgery, to wipe out infection.

By 1944, these predictions were already being confirmed. Doctors were treating war casualties with penicillin. Alec's memories of the ravages of poisoned wounds in World War I were vivid. Now he saw men still gloriously free of infection days after injury.

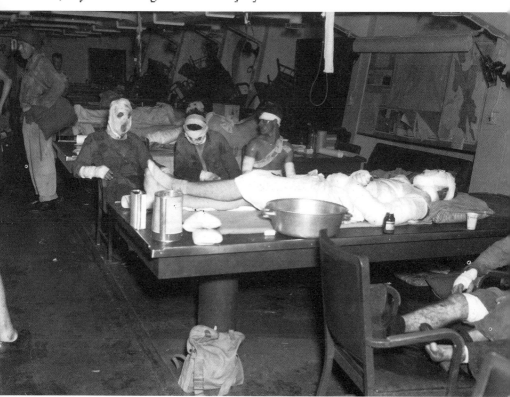

As drug companies began to make penicillin in the United States and Britain, it became available for treating war wounds. Penicillin gave men who would have had no hope in previous wars, the chance of survival from infection. It saved limbs and it saved lives, beyond counting.

Fame

Within days of Harry Lambert's cure in the summer of 1942, the news had reached the newspapers. The tremendous results in Oxford had attracted little publicity, but now the story broke. Reporters, hungry for good news in the grim years of the war, besieged St. Mary's in an effort to learn more of this wonderful new substance that could save lives.

From this moment on, Alexander Fleming was no longer a private individual. He shot to fame, and the story of penicillin's discovery, much enriched by the tale of Alec's boyhood in the wilds of Scotland, captured the public imagination.

It was also much embellished by fantasy: there was a story in one paper of how Alec found it on mouldy cheese he had eaten which cured a boil on his neck! Another, grandly ignoring the years between 1928 and World War II, told the tale of bomb dust carrying the miracle into Alec's laboratory.

"The great strides in understanding natural phenomena are the result of the labours of thousands of people, some of whom are good scientists – and some not so good. Their combined labours might be likened to the Pointillists who applied little dabs of colour to the canvas and built up a beautiful picture. Scientists can, with luck, from time to time, put a nice dab of colour on a metaphorical canvas; but, for the elaboration of the finished work, they are dependent on the activities of thousands of colleagues."
Howard Florey, 1966.

In 1945, Alexander Fleming was awarded the Nobel Prize for Medicine, jointly with Howard Florey and Ernst Chain. He was sixty-four, and the award crowned thirty-nine years in the search for weapons against infection. With the world fame that penicillin brought him, his life changed. In answer to invitations from all over the world, he toured as an ambassador for science and medicine. He told of penicillin, of the war against bacteria, and enjoyed with undisguised pleasure the mounting evidence of pencillin's impact on people's lives throughout the world.

api 20E

ONPG	ADH	LDC	ODC	|CIT|	H2S	URE	TDA	IND	[V

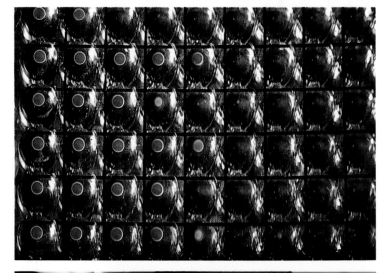

Right: Another modern method of testing for bacteria: here different substances are added to samples of blood serum in the little plastic wells, and the resulting changes are assessed.

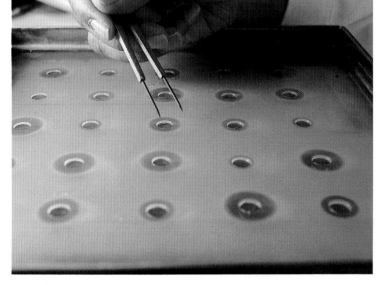

Bottom right: A method of testing preparations of varying antibiotic strength. Wells have been cut in the culture medium and filled with the antibiotic. The effect is assessed by the size of the bacteria-free zone around each well. Fleming often used this kind of technique.

GEL GLU MAN INO SOR RHA SAC MEL AMY ARA

Florey disliked this kind of publicity. He also feared that it would create a demand for penicillin among civilians, when he could not yet produce enough to supply them. He turned the reporters away, and it was only the name of Alexander Fleming that became inseparably linked with penicillin in the minds of people across the world.

Florey, Chain, or the Oxford team were sometimes briefly referred to in newspaper reports, but more often not. Or they were wrongly described as part of Alec's research. Even today many accounts of penicillin obscure the crucial role played by the Oxford scientists in giving penicillin to the world.

Alec laughed at the wilder inaccuracies of what he called the "Fleming myth", and began to keep a book of choice cuttings from the newspapers. Some he would pin on the noticeboard for others to have a chuckle.

The last years

The pleasure of these years was marred only by the growing ill-health of his wife, Sareen. Accounts of this period in Alec's life do not tell us exactly what the illness was. All we know is that, at first, she accompanied Alec on all his tours. But by 1948 she was too exhausted to continue. Alec and his son Robert watched helplessly as she became weaker and weaker. She died on October 28, 1949.

Alec was devastated. She had been his companion, friend and pillar of his home life for thirty-four years. Her death left him very much alone. The door of his laboratory, usually always open to visitors, was firmly shut. He seemed suddenly much

Bacteriologists must be sure that particular bacteria are responsible for an illness, and that the chosen antibiotic weapon will work. Nowadays, tests to identify bacteria often come ready-made from commercial laboratories.

Above: Here a microbe found in a patient's saliva has been put into each of the small wells, which contain various substances. The effect of these substances on the microbes tells the bacteriologist exactly which microbe it is. When this strip was prepared, all the wells were clear. Now, eight hours later, major changes in coloration have taken place.

57

Opposite: Alexander Fleming, carried by cheering students at his election as Rector of Edinburgh University in 1952. It was an award in his native Scotland which gave him particular pleasure. In the last ten years of his life he was given awards by leading scientific institutions all over the world, welcomed by presidents and prime-ministers, monarchs and religious leaders. All over the world people rushed to welcome the benefactor who had given new hope in the endless struggle against disease.

older than his sixty-eight years.

Only slowly did his interest in his work pull him from the misery, and he resumed something of his old spirit.

A young Greek scientist, Dr. Amalia Voureka, had joined Alec's laboratory after the war. In the years after the loss of Sareen, she became a valued companion, and she and Alec were married in 1953. At the age of seventy-four, Alec was still working in the laboratory and still able to travel. He continued until the day of his death. He died very suddenly, on March 11, 1955, of a heart attack.

The penicillin legacy

Many doctors believe that penicillin is the greatest single medical advance the world has ever known. Before the 1940s, hospitals were full of people with easily-caught infections raging out of control. After the 1940s, the tragedy of damaged health or death from common infections was a thing of the past.

Penicillin not only cured people so overwhelmed by bacteria that they were dying: it gave doctors the power to stop bacteria ever taking such a hold in the first place.

The road forward was not without problems. It soon became clear that penicillin was generally a very safe drug, but some people do become sensitive to it. These few could have severe, sometimes fatal reactions. And, just as Alec had predicted, some bacteria developed resistance to penicillin.

In Oxford, Howard Florey went on, pushing back new frontiers in the search for other antibiotics to deal with the penicillin-resistant bacteria. He added a second triumph to his career by revealing antibiotics made from other moulds to combat penicillin-defying bacteria. The new drugs could also be used on people allergic to penicillin.

Many different types of penicillin can now be produced, specially structured for particular infections, and given by mouth as well as injection. Some combat many more varieties of bacteria than the original drug.

Chance, and the prepared mind

Alec's discovery of penicillin, and of lysozyme, are examples of chance happenings superbly turned to scientific riches.

Pasteur once said, "In the field of experimentation chance favours the prepared mind." There is no more vivid evidence than the story of Alexander Fleming's two scientific gifts to the world.

There was the chance arrival of a rare strain of a mould, on a dish of bacteria believed to be invulnerable to attack. It was greeted by the trained, perceptive and curious mind of a scientist who let no observation go by without looking more closely.

He often said, "I did not invent penicillin. Nature did that. I only discovered it by accident." But his preparedness of mind, sharpened by years in the quest for a perfect antiseptic, prompted him to notice, record, investigate, and preserve a strain of mould almost unique in its ability. It was fifteen years and thousands of mould investigations later before another strain of *penicillium* with such powers was discovered.

The story of penicillin is rich in other ways. It reflects the many facets of scientific skill and effort by which the world's knowledge advances, pieced together by many people working in different ways and at different times, but all adding to the growth of understanding.

On the one hand there are the disciplined, planned efforts of a group such as the Oxford team under Florey. Each member brought their special skills to the whole; each had a central aim firing all their efforts – to develop a substance for safe systemic use in the human body.

On the other hand there is Fleming with years of accumulated understanding of bacteria and the destruction they caused. And there is his untiring, wide-ranging and unbiased investigation of all observations, his alertness of mind to things which seemed "interesting".

The fascination of the penicillin story lies not only in our knowledge of how the first antibiotic changed the world, but also in understanding these qualities in the scientists who gave it to us.

"All of us, in our ordinary pursuits, can do research, and valuable research, by continual and critical observation. If something unusual happens, we should think about it and try to find out what it means.... There can be little doubt that the future of humanity depends greatly on the freedom of the researcher to pursue his own line of thought. It is not an unreasonable ambition in a research-worker that he should become famous, but the man who undertakes research with the ultimate aim of wealth or power is in the wrong place..."

Alexander Fleming.

Important Dates

1860s   Louis Pasteur's work shows that disease is caused by living organisms. Led by Pasteur, scientists in later years discover that it is possible to inject a vaccine, the slightly weakened microbe of a disease, into a person. This encourages the body to build up an immunity to that disease.

1867   Lister realizes that bacteria are the cause of infections and uses *carbolic acid* to clean wounds and equipment from microbes.

1881   Aug 6: Alexander Fleming is born, four miles from Darvel, Scotland.

1884   Elie Metchnikoff shows the white blood cells of the blood swallowing and digesting bacteria.

1895   Alexander, or Alec, moves to London to finish his schooling while staying with his brother, Tom.

1897   Alec begins work as a shipping clerk in the City of London.

1901   Alec passes the entrance examination for St. Mary's Hospital Medical School, London.

1906   July: Alec passes his final medical school exams. In the summer he joins Almroth Wright's department at St. Mary's Hospital.

1909   At the age of twenty-seven, Alec passes his surgeon exams but decides to stay on in Wright's department.

1910   Paul Ehrlich, a German, discovers "606" or "Salvarsan", which is poisonous to the bacteria which cause syphilis. Alec becomes well-known for his treatment of syphilis.

1914   World War I begins. Almroth Wright's team, including Fleming, goes to Boulogne, France to treat the troops in appalling conditions.

1915   Dec 23: While on leave Alec marries Sally McElroy (who is later known as "Sareen"). He is thirty-four.

1919   Alec returns to London.

1921   Sareen and Alec buy their house, "The Dhoon", in Suffolk.

1921   Nov 21: Alec's notes show the beginnings of his first important discovery, lysozyme.

1924   A son, Robert, is born to the Flemings.

1928   Sept: Alec discovers the penicillium mould. In the same year he becomes Professor of Bacteriology in St. Mary's Hospital Medical School.

1929   Feb: Alec calls his new discovery "penicillin".

1935   Gerhard Domagk discovers a dye called "Prontosil" which, when swallowed or injected, kills the streptococci bacteria in mice. This leads to similar substances, known as *sulphonamides,* being developed which kill certain bacteria, but not all and not without side effects.

1940   March: Ernst Chain, of the Oxford team, extracts enough penicillin, as a brown powder, to test on animals.
        May 25: Howard Florey successfully injects the penicillin into five mice.
        Sept 2: Fleming sees the Oxford work on penicillin for the first time.

1941   The "factory" at the Dunn School has produced enough penicillin to plan the first test on a human.
Feb 12: Albert Alexander is treated with the penicillin by the Oxford team for a rose bush scratch.
March 15: Albert Alexander dies. But further human trials by the Oxford team are successful.

1942   Aug 6: Fleming injects penicillin into Harry Lambert's spinal fluid and he makes a miraculous full recovery.
Second human trials by the team in Oxford are successful.

1944   July: Fleming is knighted for his discovery of penicillin; he is now Sir Alexander Fleming. Howard Florey is also knighted for the development of penicillin as a drug.
The first of the new antibiotics after penicillin, streptomycin, is developed. It has been followed by the development of antibiotics from many other moulds.

1945   Fleming, aged forty-four, Chain and Florey are jointly awarded the Nobel Prize for Medicine.

1946   Fleming becomes Director of the Inoculation Department at St. Mary's Hospital, London, when Almroth Wright retires.

1949   Oct 28: Sareen Fleming dies of a mysterious illness.

1953   Fleming marries Amalia Voureka.

1955   March 11: Sir Alexander Fleming dies of a heart attack; he is aged seventy-four.

Further Reading

Durie, Bruce: *Medicine,* Macdonald & Co. (Educational), 1987.
Hughes, Howard W: *Alexander Fleming and Penicillin,* Priory Press Limited, 1974.
Macfarlane, Gwyn: *Alexander Fleming: The Man and the Myth,* Chatto and Windus, 1984. [This is an adult book but as it deals with the Fleming myth and gives due credit to the Oxford team, it is essential modern reading.]
Sully, Nina: *Looking at Medicine,* Batsford Educational, 1984.

Scientific Terms

Abscess: A collection of pus which is a result of the collection of *bacteria* at the site.

Antibiotic: A type of medicine made from a microbe which destroys other microbes. Penicillin, for example.

Antiseptic: A chemical substance used to destroy microbes.

Bacillus (plural bacilli): Rod-shaped *bacteria*.

Bacteria (singular bacterium) : One kind of microbe – microscopic organisms which are too small to be seen with the naked eye. The people who study them are bacteriologists.

Coma: A state of unconsciousness from which a person cannot be roused.

Culture: The artificial growth of *micro-organisms*, especially *bacteria*, in a prepared culture dish.

Epidemic: The spread of a disease to a region, affecting large numbers of people, when the disease is not normally present in that area.

Incubate: To keep something at the right temperature to encourage its growth.

Immune: The state of being resistant to microbes of a particular disease. The body's immune system creates immunity.

Inoculate: To plant a disease in a person or animal by introducing microbes or a *virus* in order to force the body to develop its *immunity* to it.

Lysozyme: The body's natural *antiseptic*, a substance which is found in our tears, mucus, saliva, pus, blood serum and in some plants, which fights against infection by microbes.

Meningitis: Inflammation of the membranes which surround the brain and the spinal cord, caused by infection by microbes.

Micro-organism: A microscopic (ie too small to be seen with the naked eye) living creature.

Phagocytes: The white blood cells able to swallow and digest *bacteria* and dead cells.

Solvent: A substance, usually a liquid, which dissolves another substance. For example, in a solution of sugar and water, water is the solvent.

Staphylococcus (plural staphylococci): Round *bacterium* which grows in clumps.

Streptococcus (plural streptococci): Round *bacterium* which grows in chains.

Sulphonamides: The group of chemical drugs which killed certain types of *bacteria*. They were fairly successful but had unpleasant side effects.

Systemically: Introduced to circulate through the blood stream.

Vaccine: The slightly weakened *bacterium* or *virus* of any disease which is injected into a person or animal in order to create *immunity*.

Virulent: Extremely dangerous or poisonous. The microbe *streptococcus* is virulent and often kills people.

Virus: The smallest known microbe, much smaller than a *bacterium*.

"The research-worker must be at liberty to follow wherever a new discovery may lead him.... Every research-worker should have a certain amount of time to himself, so as to be able to work out his own ideas without having to give an account of them (unless he wants to) to anybody. Momentous things may happen in a man's free time."

Alexander Fleming.

"The research-worker is familiar with disappointment – the weary months spent in following the wrong road, the many failures. But even failures have their uses, for, properly analysed, they may lead him to success. For the man engaged in research there is no joy equal to that of discovery, no matter how unimportant it may be. That is what keeps him going...."

Alexander Fleming.

Index